Why *Quiet Spaces*?

Chairman of BRF's board of trustees, Bishop Colin Fletcher, looks at the motivation behind our new publishing venture.

Speak of spirituality and a glazed look comes across many people's eyes. All too easily it becomes one of those words that means, as Humpty Dumpty puts it in Alice through the Looking Glass, 'just what I choose it to mean—neither more nor less'.

Yet you would have to be very blind indeed to fail to see that this is an area of human experience that thousands of people see themselves as exploring at present. As institutional religion declines in this country and elsewhere in Western Europe, alternative 'spiritual' self-help books, courses, therapies and programmes seem to flourish at an ever-increasing rate.

This should come as no surprise. St Augustine summed it up beautifully when he wrote, 'You have made us for yourself, and our heart is restless till it finds its rest in you.' In other words, people will always be searching for spiritual fulfilment, though that may express itself in all kinds of ways and will ultimately only find fulfilment in a living relationship with God.

As Christians we may feel wary of non-conventional kinds of spiritual expression that disturb our own ideas of what faith demands. Sometimes we simply need to be humble enough to say that we have got a lot to learn. But there is nothing to be afraid of, and the God whom we worship encompasses every form of human experience.

The path of saying that, spiritually, 'anything goes' is unsatisfactory. God cares deeply about questions of truth and how they impact on our lives. But that still leaves us with great freedom to enter into constructive dialogue, often based as much on shared experiences as on the exchange of words.

My hope is that Quiet Spaces will provide a forum where that dialogue can take place—where people can share stories of their encounters with God, learn from one another in surprising ways and, above all else, find new pathways to respond to Jesus' invitation, 'If anyone is thirsty let him come to me and drink.' ∎

Welcome

BECKY WINTER

Welcome to the very first edition of *Quiet Spaces*, a journal of spirituality and prayer for all those who are looking for ideas and inspiration for the journey of faith. Our hope is that readers of different ages and stages, of varying church background and outlook, will find here a meeting place, an open space where we can pause and ponder.

'Creation and creativity' is a good theme for a new venture and you will see the interesting and varied ways our authors have engaged with the subject. We would love your input. If you write meditations or prayers, do calligraphy or line drawings, or have a story to tell, please write in. (See page 63 for further information.) Together, we can make *Quiet Spaces* something of lasting value.

Becky Winter

Text copyright © BRF 2005
Illustrations copyright © Jane Bottomley, Chris Daunt and Ian Mitchell
Inside front cover image © William Gray

Published by
The Bible Reading Fellowship, First Floor, Elsfield Hall, 15–17 Elsfield Way, Oxford OX2 8FG
Website: www.brf.org.uk
ISBN 1 84101 415 X

Printed by Gutenberg Press, Tarxien, Malta

Quiet Spaces

Exploring prayer & spirituality

Quiet Spaces

In the beginning...
DAVID WINTER explores...

You say you're NOT creative!
Sue Atkinson says you are!

Margaret Silf
encourages us to step into space

Creation's window on suffering
JEAN WATSON reflects on her own experience

Creation and creativity

CONTENTS

PLUS our regular features:
Prayer through the week, meditations and reflections, poems and quotes

Spirituality
—the search for meaning

Alison Webster is Social Responsibility Adviser for the Diocese of Oxford.

> Can we afford to live imaginatively, contemplatively? Why have we submitted to a society that tries to make imagination a privilege when to each of us it comes as a birthright?
>
> JEANETTE WINTERSON

Apparently within hours of the tragic train crash at Ladbroke Grove in October 1999, passers-by had begun to place flowers on the road bridge that passed over the railway line nearest to the crash. As time went by, bouquets accumulated, including some from relatives and friends of those who had died. Sometimes, families of those killed on our roads turn the fatality sites into roadside shrines, tying flowers and soft toys to lamp posts and road signs. When there are major disasters, such activity causes much angst to those in local authority emergency planning departments who are charged with deciding what to do with the mementos (if that is what they are)—how to 'dispose of them' in an appropriate manner. To know that, you've got to understand what's at stake—what is their significance. And no one is really quite sure. On anniversaries of such tragedies, symbols appear again. Remember how we were encouraged on the anniversary of the Dunblane shootings to light a candle and place it in our window?

Some have argued that we have, as human beings, a kind of 'essential spiritual core' transcending time and place, manifesting itself differently according to circumstance. Whether or not that is true, I would argue that in extreme circumstances, when meaninglessness and futility threaten to overwhelm order and rationality, human beings need forms of linguistic and symbolic expression that speak of mystery, meaning and transcendence in ways that connect with, but go beyond, everyday speech. In our contemporary context, the word 'spirituality' functions as a catch-all signifier of this largely unarticulated need. Health and sickness, birth and death, are, of course, life experiences that call forth both the need for and the possibility of such forms of expression.

'a good thing' all the same? Does it fit with groups of young women sitting on the grass at Kensington Gardens, meditating around a candle, with masses of flowers? Or is it more to do with the angry coming to terms with the impending death of the terminally ill person who recognizes she has not got long to go? Or is it the mood of calm engendered by communion brought to the bedside, or the lighting of Sabbath candles? Or is it all of these things?[1]

The sacred... has left us without leaving us alone

JULIA KRISTEVA

Defining spirituality

Various attempts have been made to define and pin down 'the spiritual' in order to facilitate policy making in this arena, but clarity has so far proved elusive. Rabbi Julia Neuberger, formerly Chief Executive of the King's Fund, has summed up the difficulties as follows:

Is 'spirituality' that sense of 'the other' we heard so many people describe at the time of the death of Princess Diana? Is it somewhat mawkish and sentimental, ill thought-through—but

Let us explore some of the other definitions that have been offered. The National Schizophrenia Fellowship, now called 'Rethink', has a policy statement on 'meeting the spiritual needs of people with a severe mental illness' which deploys the following definition of spirituality:

It's a quality that goes beyond religious affiliation, that strives for inspiration, reverence, awe, meaning and purpose, even in those who do not believe in any god. The spiritual dimension tries

5

to be in harmony with the universe, strives for answers about the infinite and comes into focus when a person faces emotional illness, physical illness and death.

Another writer, David Lyall, turns to the nursing literature for help. He discovers Linda Ross, who has defined the spiritual dimension as 'that element within the individual from which originates: meaning, purpose and fulfilment in life; a will to live; belief and faith in self, others and God and which is essential to the attainment of an optimum state of health, well-being or quality of life'. Another author cited by David Lyall speaks of spirituality as being characterized by 'interconnectedness and self-transcendence'.[2]

Stephen Pattison, a writer in my own field of theology, has given systematic attention to analysing the development of the concept of spirituality in healthcare contexts. He says:

'Spirituality' is often used as a more inclusive substitute for the word religion. Definitions are various, fluid and imprecise. Spirituality can be understood as that aspect of human existence which relates to structures of significance that give meaning and direction to a person's life and help them deal with the vicissitudes of existence. It is associated with the human quest for meaning, purpose, self-transcending knowledge, meaningful relationships, love and a sense of the holy. It may, or may not, be associated with a specific religious system.[3]

Spirituality, then, is to be understood as distinct from and going beyond organized and institutionalized religious systems and traditions. Belief in God is not necessary to it, though belief itself is, but this can encompass a belief in a variety of things: the harmony of the universe; the

Spirituality...

… a quality that goes beyond religious affiliation, that strives for inspiration, reverence, awe, meaning and purpose…

possibility of self-transcendence; meaningful relationships; a meaning and purpose to life. Spirituality is variously perceived as essential to optimum well-being or as that which comes into focus mainly at times of crisis. In his characteristically caustic style, Pattison sums up the functioning of the concept as follows:

> There has been a recent explosion of interest in people's happiness and well-being

Notions of 'spirituality' that are presently in play are diffuse, vague and contradictory. 'Spirituality' seems to function like intellectual polyfilla, changing shape and content conveniently to fill the space its users devise for it. Having mostly departed from the theories and practices of religion, theorists and practitioners of spirituality are muddled about what actually constitutes their subject matter.[4]

What makes for well-being?

There has been a recent explosion of interest in people's happiness and well-being, particularly on the part of government.[5] This has been sparked by the devastating research finding that while economic output has nearly doubled in the last 30 years, life satisfaction in the UK has remained flat. In his 2003 Lionel Robbins Memorial Lectures, economist Richard Layard looked at levels of life satisfaction in the UK from 1973 to 2002 and summed up the findings:

It is striking that the level of life satisfaction in the UK has been remarkably flat—averaging 6.9 on a scale of 0–10. So despite GDP per person increasing by over 80 per cent in real terms since the 1970s, people's satisfaction with their lives has not really changed at all in 30 years.'[6]

I suggest that the 'spirituality' agenda is about an agenda of frustration with the predominant values of a 'money culture'. Is not the current interest in 'work/life balance' a manifestation of this rejection of the money culture in favour of living life more imaginatively—or, at least, with more integration?

Novelist and social commentator Jeanette Winterson, in her book Art Objects, has reflected powerfully on the nature of art, imagination and the human spirit, and I think her

> Spirituality does
> not begin in an
> empty place;
> it does not hang
> in mid-air or drift
> aimlessly. It arises
> in a given context,
> is based on
> certain values…
>
> CATHARINA J.M. HALKES

renewed it needs its own coin.'[7] She continues her sharp critique of 'money culture' as follows:

Money culture recognizes no currency but its own. Whatever is not money, whatever is not making money, is useless to it. The entire efforts of our government as directed through our society are efforts towards making more and more money. This favours the survival of the dullest. This favours those who prefer to live in a notional reality where goods are worth more than time and where things are more important than ideas.[8]

Winterson calls to our attention the need to recognize and prioritize the imaginative life and the arts because, in her words, 'the arts stimulate and satisfy a part of our nature that would otherwise be left untouched… the emotions art arouses in us are of a different order to those aroused by experience of any other kind'.[9] She speaks prophetically, inspiring us to see art not as an add-on luxury, important to human well-being only after all our material needs have been met, but as necessity; she inspires us to see art as very much like religion:

Art is visionary; it sees beyond the view from the window, even though the window is its frame. This is why the arts fare much better alongside religion than alongside either capitalism or communism. The god-instinct and the art-instinct both apprehend more than the physical

reflections are relevant here in talking of spirituality as being about alternative ways of living. She says, 'I do not think it an exaggeration to say that most of the energy of most of the people is being diverted into a system which destroys them. Money is no antidote. If the imaginative life is to be

biological material world. The artist need not believe in God, but the artist does consider reality as multiple and complex.[10]

The ultimate implication is that the well-being brought about by art is not an easy well-being, but a most challenging one: 'Art is not documentary... its true effort is to open to us dimensions of the spirit and of the self that normally lie smothered under the weight of living.'[11] And again, 'We know we are dissatisfied, but the satisfactions that we seek come at a price beyond the resources of a money culture. Can we afford to live imaginatively, contemplatively? Why have we submitted to a society that tries to make imagination a privilege when to each of us it comes as a birthright?'[12]

These are the questions that an engagement with 'spirituality' aims to address. ■

This article is a shortened version of a paper given at a Roffey Park conference, 'Spirit at Work', in April 2003, based on Alison's book Wellbeing, published by SCM Press.

NOTES

1 J. Neuberger, Foreword in H. Orchard (ed.), *Spirituality in Health Care Contexts*, JKP, 2001, p. 7.
2 D. Lyall, 'Spiritual Institutions' in H. Orchard (ed.), *Spirituality in Health Care Contexts*, JKP, 2000, 47–56, p. 49.
3 J. Swinton and S. Pattison, 'Come all ye faithful', *Health Service Journal*, Thursday 20 December 2001, 24–25, p. 24.
4 S. Pattison, 'Dumbing Down the Spirit' in H. Orchard (ed.), *Spirituality in Health Care Contexts*, JKP, 2001, 33–46, p. 37.
5 See, for example, 'Life Satisfaction: the state of knowledge and implications for government', December 2002, by Nick Donovan and David Halpern, Cabinet Office Strategy Unit, and 'The power and potential of well-being indicators: Measuring young people's well-being in Nottingham', New Economics Foundation and Nottinghamshire County Council, 2004.
6 From lecture 1, 'What is Happiness? Are we getting happier?', Lionel Robbins Memorial Lectures, by Richard Layard, March 2003, London School of Economics.
7 J. Winterson, *Art Objects: Essays on Ecstasy and Effrontery*, Vintage, 1996, p. 135.
8 Winterson, *Art Objects*, p. 138
9 Winterson, *Art Objects*, p. 135.
10 Winterson, *Art Objects*, p. 136.
11 Winterson, *Art Objects*, p. 138.
12 Winterson, *Art Objects*, p. 139.

In the beginning, GOD...

Canon David Winter is a writer, speaker and broadcaster. He is a General Editor for BRF's 'People's Bible Commentary' series and has written many popular books. His most recent book is 'Making Sense of the Bible' (Lion Publishing).

Like all good stories, the Bible's one has a beginning. Not 'Once upon a time'—because, before the creation, time didn't exist—but simply 'In the beginning'. Human beings have always been fascinated by origins, and none more so than those who live in our present scientific age. We want to know where it all comes from, partly because that might help to answer the question 'Where's it all going to?' The title of the Bible's first book, Genesis, is a Greek word linked to our word 'genealogy', and implies an account of human origins. Its Hebrew name, on the other hand, which is simply the first words of the text ('In the beginning' or 'When first') truly speaks of the origin of everything. Before, there was 'formless void'... and God.

Without God, we are searching for nothing beyond what we already have, which is ourselves

In the beginning when God created the heavens and the earth, the earth was a formless void and darkness covered the face of the deep, while a wind from God swept over the face of the waters. Then God said, 'Let there be light', and there was light. And God saw that the light was good; and God separated the light from the darkness.
GENESIS 1:1–4 (NRSV)

That is the real message of these opening chapters of the Bible. In the beginning, there was God... and nothing else. No biblical writer argues for the existence of God: it is simply taken as self-evident. As the Creed says, he is the 'maker of all that is, seen and unseen'. All of the Bible's story moves on from that opening premise: God, and God alone, is the source of light and life and love. At his word, light shines in the darkness. At his breath, 'the man' receives life. By his touch, the companion is brought into being, 'the woman', and the mystery of human love is created at the will of divine love.

No spirituality that is not built on this foundational principle can offer us long-term satisfaction. God alone is the source of light, life and love. He has made us and we are his. Consequently, apart from him we can never fulfil our potential as human beings, 'made in the image of God' (Genesis 1:27). If we want to seek for 'ourselves', the search really ought to start with our origin, and that is the Creator.

In the beginning, the Word...

The phrase 'in the beginning' also occurs, of course, in the New Testament, in the opening words of John's Gospel, in what is obviously intended to be an echo of the opening words of Genesis. This time, however, it is not 'In the beginning, God' but 'In the beginning was the Word'. Clearly the writer didn't intend to contradict the Hebrew scriptures, which were deeply revered by the first Christians as well as the Jewish people, so the logical deduction is that 'God' and 'the Word' are one and the same—the very point John goes on to make.

That 'Word'—logos in Greek—'became flesh' (John 1:14), and clearly the writer is thinking of Jesus Christ. Logos means more than a 'word' in the dictionary sense. There is a Greek word for that—rhema. Logos is revelation, meaning, even explanation. The God of creation has now fully 'explained' himself, by 'pitching his tent among us', the literal translation of John's phrase. In other words, at the heart of truth is a Creator-God and a 'Word' who makes him known.

God, and God alone, is the source of light and life and love

11

A truly Christian spirituality

> If we want to seek for 'ourselves', the search really ought to start with our origin, and that is the Creator

If all that sounds very mysterious (which it is), its implications for a truly Christian spirituality are quite simple. Just as no true spirituality can exist apart from God the Creator, so must it take into account God the Word. If it is not centred on God and Jesus, it is certainly less than a Christian spirituality, and possibly less than truly 'spiritual' at all.

I suppose what I am saying is that a completely secular spirituality must, by its very nature, be based entirely on human feelings, needs and emotions, without reference to the source of humanity. That's not to say that such an exercise is completely valueless, simply that it is less than the real thing. A spirituality that doesn't recognize both that we are creatures—not self-made, not cosmic accidents—and that we are flawed and liable to self-delusion and in need of a Saviour will never fully address our real nature as human beings.

Of course we employ our God-given senses in our search for true spirituality. We use eyes, ears, touch and smell as we search for signs of the Creator in the objects of his creation. In that search we also seek to find deeper truths about ourselves, about our needs, hopes, fears and longings. In silence we strain to catch the echo of the divine voice. In prayer we cry out for glimpses of the eternal. All of this is the working material of the spiritual life.

And all of it flows from the first great act of creation, or, more precisely, from the God who brought it about. Without him, we are searching for nothing beyond what we already have, which is ourselves. With him, and with the Word who came to 'make him known', we can enter into unimaginable realms of the Spirit. ■

*Creator God,
You are the
potter.
I am the clay.
I am the work
of your hands.
I am the clay.
You are the
potter.
Shape in me
your plans.
Amen*

PRAYER

What is creativity?

Jean Watson sets the scene

In the Bible, God is shown first of all as creative—as a multi-talented artistic genius, to put it in inadequate human terms. At the very least he must have enjoyed producing and playing with all kinds of materials and designing our utterly amazing, varied, interconnected universe. Like all works of creativity, it reveals some of his attributes.

And God made us in his image. Part of what that means is that he made us capable of responding to and reflecting something of his creatvity. As Christians growing into our full humanity, we have all the resources we need for realizing that potential.

Creativity in its broadest sense can be said to be an attitude, a way of responding to God, life, everything. It means realizing the possibilities given to us by God within our world and our personalities in love and freedom. Full creativity means being new people, sharing Christ's resurrection life.

Artistic creativity, though, is just one aspect of this much wider concept. We can express our creativity in every area of life. Imagination, which lies at the heart of all creativity, equips us to live life seeing beyond the obvious, it helps us to probe and explore, to seek fresh possibilities. Viewed in this way, creativity is about a way of seeing things and can help us to discover meaning in what at first seemed meaningless, discover connections where none seemed to exist, and provide us with the vision to challenge the mediocre, drab and shallow. ■

So why creativity?

- Because God is creative.
- Because it's a way of being fully human as created, redeemed and indwelt by God.
- Because it opens up truth for us in new and deeper ways.

Three weeks ago, I read an e-mail from someone in an online Christian writing group that was exploring the reason for living. 'My evangelical friends would say that the reason for living is to evangelize.' I was stunned. Surely not? The image came into my mind of the earnest person on a street corner shouting about repentance and holding up their much-thumped Bible.

A few hours later, others in the e-mail group began to say that the purpose of living was to 'glorify God and enjoy him for ever'. Yes, that made more sense to me, but it still didn't quite connect with some of the thoughts that whirled through my mind following on from that initial e-mail.

Maybe, for me, the purpose of living is much closer to the idea of being salt and light in the world, and finding ways to seek spiritual freedom and to live in harmony with creation.

- Salt in the world: it is unseen, but so necessary.
- Light in the world: the source of all life, for without light no plant will grow, and with no plants no animals could exist.

Creative? Me?

Exploring our innate creativity

Sue Atkinson is an author and speaker who is well-known for her work in the area of depression and self-esteem. Her book 'Climbing out of Depression' has been widely acclaimed and has stayed in print for over a decade.

Seeking spiritual freedom

When I have been trying to struggle free of some life crisis —for example, recovering from deep depression, or finding a way forward after bereavement —and when I have observed others trying to do the same, it seems that doing something creative can be the key to our long-term spiritual and mental well-being.

I will hastily add here that doing something creative is not necessarily doing an amazing painting good enough to put on the wall. It is much more about trying to live in harmony with creation and rediscovering within ourselves the creative spark that, I am a hundred per cent sure, is present in every human being. For many of us, the criticisms and cruelties of parents, teachers and other children long stamped on that spark and we taught ourselves the language of:

- Creative? Me? No chance— I'm hopeless.
- I thought I might be more creative in my life but now I'm too stressed and busy.
- I did write poetry once, but I know it is no good.

These are signs that we are trapped in a spiritual whirlpool that can only suck us down into more stress and loss of emotional and spiritual freedom. We are not being our true selves as God intended. We have not learnt the real meaning of recreation as an essential part of the rhythms of life.

The first faltering steps to freedom

We were made in the image of God the Creator, ready for fun and play (why else would God have made fjords and mountains and puffins if not

...glorify God and enjoy him for ever...

for the sheer fun and pleasure of it?) and I believe that we are most God-like when we are creative.

The first step along this journey is to look carefully at those hammer blows that have all but extinguished our creative spark, and learn to let go of those hurts.

I was told, 'How can you possibly be a writer? You can't even spell'; 'You can't draw— that looks stupid', and so on.

Then in adult life came those oddly pretentious comments such as, 'Well, of course, it's not real literature'. The things that made you lose sight of your creativity might be very different from my things, but identifying them and saying 'stuff what others think' is in itself a huge creative move.

Living in harmony with creation

Our lives are just a tiny part of our universe, but they have huge significance. We join with God in:

- the play of creation and the sheer wonder at the freshness of the green as the buds on the trees down the road burst on a sunny spring day (so we might creatively play in our garden or grow herbs for neighbours).
- soaking in the resurrection life as daffodils smile at us and we see the first butterfly (and resurrection joy of life permeates everything we do, from the colours of the clothes we wear to the choice of fair trade and local products when we shop).
- letting ourselves be a part of the amazing life around us and allowing ourselves to feel astonishment when we look closely at a sunflower head, as well catching a falling leaf and letting our thoughts wander towards the death and quiet of winter (so we respect our environment and use resources sensitively).
- the multicoloured joy of creation and care for those around us ('when I was sick you visited me')

Creativity unpacked

We do need to see creativity as something much wider than what some people might call 'high art'. Art galleries are full of stunning beauty (and some interesting thoughts on art, such as an unmade bed). The great message that Tracey

Emin's unmade bed gives me is that I am one of the greatest artists of the world!

But our creativity is the spark at the centre of our life, and might be expressed by:

- the way we have the lighting and furniture in a room.
- our photos.
- our sense of colour as we make a meal.
- lighting a lavender candle when someone is stressed and needing some love and care.
- keeping a 'memory box' or scrapbook of the little things that make up our lives.
- writing a birthday story for someone we love.
- sending a simple message on a post card.
- singing nursery rhymes to a small child.
- any number of other things that we do in our ordinary everyday life.

A journey towards God

Creativity is so deep within all of us that our journey is about discovering something that was there in us all the time. It is a journey towards finding pleasure and contentment in every aspect of our life and valuing ourselves enough to use our creativity to the full.

God said 'It is good' when creating, and that is our aim. So decorating a room or planting a native hedge for the birds or writing a poem might not come up to our perfectionist standards (and we might even groan when we stand back to look at what we have done!) but we have used that creative spark; we have moved on; we have walked into the unknown with God.

It is a journey towards finding pleasure and contentment in every aspect of our life and valuing ourselves enough to use our creativity to the full

I really believe that God smiles just as much at the crooked shelves we made as at the most deeply felt, hearty singing of a great hymn in a packed and joyful church.

Valuing ourselves

We might not be able to paint a portrait, and might think ourselves of less value than those who can. But learning that we are unique and of

This spacious firmament on high,
With all the blue ethereal sky,
And spangled heavens, a shining frame,
Their great original proclaim.
The unwearied sun, from day to day,
Does his Creator's power display;
And publishes to every land
The work of an almighty hand...

What though in solemn silence all
Move round this dark terrestrial ball;
What though no real voice or sound
Amid their radiant orbs be found:
In reason's ear they all rejoice,
And utter forth a glorious voice,
For ever singing as they shine:
'The hand that made us is divine!'

JOSEPH ADDISON (1672–1719)

inestimable value to our Creator is one of the great life journeys. We move on from our low self-esteem and find our true value, playing on the carpet with a small child, whittling an alligator out of a bit of a stick, or expressing our sadness at death in a poem, even if we dare not show it to anyone—yet!

So what is the purpose of life?

Maybe it is evangelism! Doesn't that mean sharing the good news? Doesn't it mean laughing, dancing and sharing with a creator God who wants us to enjoy a life of glorious freedom to re-create, to experience contentment and pleasure that can sustain us and others through all that life throws at us. Creative? Me? Yes, you. ■

Painting
our Prayers…

Kate Litchfield is a diocesan counsellor and Wendy Shaw is awaiting ordination. As artists, both have been exploring the interface between spirituality, art and healing over many years, and praying through painting has become central to their spiritual journeys. They have recently established 'Burning Bush— Praying with a Visual Voice', an initiative to encourage and enable prayer and worship through creative visual art in the Diocese of Norwich.

All of them were filled with the Holy Spirit and began to speak in other languages as the Spirit gave them ability.

ACTS 2:4 (NRSV)

… is praying with our eyes open!

To touch our creativity is to touch our divinity

MEISTER ECKHART

You don't have to be good at art to paint your prayers! Praying through painting involves painting expressively and spontaneously without trying to make 'successful' paintings. It uses the language of colour, mark, line, shape and pattern instead of the language of words. It is about painting from our inner landscape, instead of the landscape we see in the world around us.

Some experiences of life and faith take us beyond words and we may need another language to express all that lies deep within us. We may not even be aware of what is hidden there in the centre of our being, where we encounter God, but prayer painting can help us to connect with this inner landscape and give it form.

Jesus communicated in creative ways that could be felt and seen, scribbling in the sand and mixing mud and spit. And God communicates with

19

us through our creativity; we receive and respond through our imagination, sustained and enriched by faith.

Likewise the Spirit helps us in our weakness; for we do not know how to pray as we ought, but that very Spirit intercedes with sighs too deep for words.
ROMANS 8:26 (NRSV)

Taking the risk to choose to let go and be vulnerable with watercolour, paper and brush is leading me to try to take the risk to let go more and be more open and vulnerable in my prayer and meditation... I found that I didn't die when I made that risk... To the contrary, I became very much more alive.

MARILLA BARGHUSEN (QUOTED IN 'ORIGINAL BLESSING' BY MATTHEW FOX)

Letting go... is letting God!

You don't have to get it right to paint your prayers! There are no rules or standards about how prayer paintings should look. The images can be abstract or representational. At first, painting this way may feel risky, because we do not feel in control of the outcome. But prayer also means letting go of control, taking risks and allowing ourselves to be led by God into new and unknown places. So our prayer paintings may turn out to be mysterious, raw, funny, confusing, joyous or challenging.

All sorts of materials are suitable for prayer painting—poster or ready-mixed paints, watercolour in tubes or pans, acrylic or oil paints, soft pastels, oil pastels, coloured crayons or fibre-tip pens. Buy one or two items to try out first. Use inexpensive materials from discount stores or children's art suppliers. Mail order and online stores offer good bargains. Paint on anything from brown wrapping paper, or pages of unwanted books, to quality watercolour and cartridge paper. Start a prayer painting journal in a sketchbook.

Soak it! Splodge it! Splat it! Rub it! Rip it! Brush it! Scribble it! Smudge it! Dribble it! Drop it! Stroke it! Float it! Smooth it! Blob it! Love it!

Begin your prayer painting with a time of silent prayer, a Bible reading or by asking God to be with you and guide you as you pray with paint. Then try experimenting with these suggestions, which will help you get started and free you from preconceived ideas of how to paint.

- Scribble over the paper with a white candle before painting. You can't see the marks, so will have to stop worrying about not being able to draw. The wax will resist the colours and show up as white lines on your painting.
- Use your non-dominant hand. This hand has not been taught to write carefully and will be more spontaneous and expressive.
- Scribble with a pen, crayon or pastel. Spend time looking at the scribbles until an image emerges. Experiment with mark-making, using different ways of holding the materials and different pressures.
- Wet the paper with a sponge before you begin (this works best with thick watercolour paper). Using poster paint or watercolour paint from the tube, hold a brush in each hand and load the two brushes with different coloured paints, letting the colours choose you. Paint into the wet paper with your eyes shut, letting the brushes lead your hands. Open your eyes after a couple of minutes and continue painting.

As you paint, let images, shapes and patterns emerge, and respond to them.

Work of sight is done. Now do heart work on the pictures within you.

RAINER MARIA RILKE

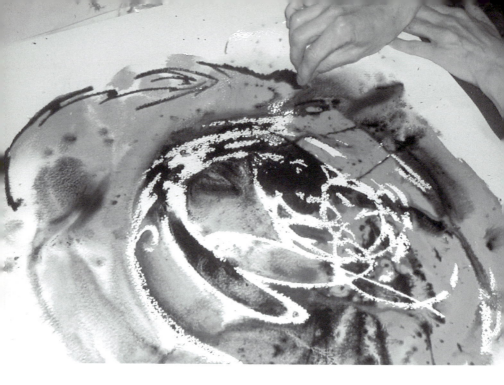

You must give birth to your images. They are the future waiting to be born... fear not the strangeness you feel. The future must enter into you long before it happens... just wait for the birth... for the hour of new clarity.

RAINER MARIA RILKE

Does the painting need something more, perhaps a particular colour, shape or mark? Does something in it attract your attention? Can you see an image forming?

Let go of expectations of how you want the prayer painting to look and let the painting lead you. Don't give up because you feel stuck. As so often with prayer, meanings may unfold as you paint your prayers, or may come later.

Let the meanings unfold... and give thanks!

After you have finished painting, sit quietly with your prayer painting and let it speak to you through colour, shape and form.

- What are the areas of energy, movement, stillness or space in your prayer painting?
- Is there an image or is it abstract?
- What do the colours mean for you? What thoughts or feelings arise in you as you look?
- Has the prayer painting experience spoken to you about your relationship with God?
- Do any words come spontaneously to mind in response to your painting? Perhaps a Bible passage?

Ask God to go on speaking to you through the colours, shape and form.

Keep your prayer paintings safely. Remember always that they are an expression of your prayer and the meaning is personal to you; share them only with those who will understand and respect this.

Be silent.
Be still.
Be waiting.
Be watching.
Be open.
Be.

See yourself
in energy, in movement, in quietness,
spaces,
meeting places,
divided,
united

in colours,

in darkness,
in light,

see God,
creation together.

SUGGESTED READING

Seeding the Spirit—the Appleseed Workbook, Chris Cook and Brenda Clifft Heales (Woodbrooke Quaker Study Centre, 2001)
Scribbling in the Sand—Christ and Creativity, Michael Card (IVP, 2002)
Art as a Way of Knowing, Pat B. Allen (Shambhala, 1995)
Visual Journaling, Barbara Ganim and Susan Fox (Quest Books, 1999)

ART SUPPLIERS

www.atlantisart.co.uk
Tel: 020 7377 8855
www.greatart.co.uk
Tel: 0845 601 5772

Both the above suppliers have an extensive range of art materials available online and by mail order at good prices.

www.artsupplies.co.uk
Tel 08453 30 32 34

Good discounts on watercolour paper, brushes and other items.

www.tummybox.com
Tel: 01924 840759

Attractive, good-value sketchbooks suitable for prayer painting journals.

For further information contact:
Kate Litchfield: katel@fish.co.uk
Wendy Shaw:
wendyjaneshaw@virgin.net

> There's no right or wrong way to pray with a colour— everyone has a different experience

Colours
for the Soul

Fleur Dorrell is Head of Prayer and Spirituality for the Mothers' Union. She has a keen interest in creativity and spirituality and leads workshops and quiet days on themes related to the arts.

Why are we attracted to different colours? Do they make us feel good? We accept and reject various colours for different reasons, but do we reflect on why this is so?

Red is positive, strong and passionate but can be seen as aggressive.

Blue is calming, safe to wear and the only colour we actually 'feel'.

Black is common to wear as it 'goes' with everything— despite its funereal connotations.

Orange/Yellow are warm colours representing fun and optimism.

White is still a sign of purity.

The English language is particularly colourful: when ill or envious we look green; if depressed we feel blue; when tired we are jaded; when embarrassed or angry we turn pink or red; when cowardly we are yellow; when we're frightened we look white; when fed up we are browned off; and sometimes people nearing death look grey. But how would we describe these colours to someone born blind?

Liturgical colours and seasons of the Church

Using colours to differentiate liturgical seasons became a common practice in the Western Church from the fourth century. By the twelfth century, Pope Innocent III had systematized the use of five colours: purple, white, black, red and green. Blue and gold have been added recently.

Purple: an ancient royal colour, as it was rare, so became a symbol of the sovereignty of Christ—also repentance from sin.
White and gold: the brightness of day.
Black: traditional colour of mourning in some cultures.
Red: blood, the colour of martyrs and of Christ's death on the cross—also fire, so the colour of the Holy Spirit.
Green: growth, used in ordinary time.
Blue: sky; in some rites it honours Mary.

Colours can be used in altar and pulpit decorations, vestments, banners, and tapestries.

Imagination and creativity are important aspects of wholeness. Both the arts and religion seek to open our

Some great books about colour

Alexander Theroux, *The Primary Colours*
Simon Garfield, *Mauve*
Michel Pastoureau, *Blue: the history of a colour*
John Gage, *Colour and Culture*
Victoria Finlay, *Travels through my Paintbox*
Ann Bird, *Colour Me Spiritual*

eyes, reveal truths and help us to see the world differently. This is why colour meditations are so powerful as means of praying: they tap into the colours that can help and heal us in ways that resonate deep down in our souls. Colours articulate our emotions and express subconscious feelings that can be triggered at a moment's notice. Colour meditations unlock feelings by bringing them to the surface for our exploration. Past events, memories and important incidences can be revealed when the right colours have triggered the events during a led meditation.

Try colour meditations at home

- Light a candle or listen to gentle music.
- Collect four to six different coloured squares or magazine images. Choose colours that you both like and dislike, ensuring a good variety of shades. Spread them out separately on a table or floor.
- Spend five minutes with each one, looking at the colours, and pray that God will speak to you through them. Let your mind wander in any direction. The colours will take you wherever they want.
- If you feel you're not getting anywhere, keep trying or go on to the next colour.

There's no right or wrong way to pray with a colour—everyone has a different experience.

Don't worry if nothing much happens as these colours will stay with you throughout the next few months; it may be later that the colours can speak to you.

If you do look at all the colours, next lay them all out closely together; reflect on them as a whole and see what happens.

Sometimes colours that we didn't like on their own look and feel much better next to other colours. This can tell us much about how we see colours and ourselves. Thank God for these colours and for what they show us about God and creation.

If you are really keen, you can then choose a painting that you like and study the colours in the painting, using the same principles but with a whole picture rather than just one colour. ■

Imagination
and creativity
are important aspects of wholeness

a meditation

Used in a group, this meditation should be read by a leader in a slow and calm way. To use it alone, the meditation should be read through and then visualized with eyes closed. Before you begin, sit for a while in a comfortable position. Try to slow your breathing and maybe focus on a candle, icon or any object of this sort. Let the words 'Be still and know that I am God' fill your mind. Say the sentence aloud or silently, simply allowing the words to flow. When you are ready and with your eyes gently closed, the meditation can begin.

Picture a snow-covered garden. Everything is covered in beautiful fresh snow. It is a scene of pure, untouched whiteness…

After a while you notice one small flower--one solitary, bold flower that has broken the whiteness. What colour is it? Concentrate on the flower, noticing its shape as well as its colour…

The sun strengthens over the snowy scene, the snow glistens, the garden is bright white. Nothing moves, everything is completely still. Around you and as far as you can see, everything is wrapped in stillness…

You look up and notice the extraordinary blueness of the cloudless sky. Above you blue, around you white and one tiny, courageous flower. The peace is profound. Let this peace surround you and envelop you. Enjoy the stillness. Enjoy God's peace, the deep peace of God surrounding and enveloping you…

Gently leave the scene, taking a sense of God's presence with you. ■

Seeing in the dark

Margaret Silf is an ecumenical Christian, trained by the Jesuits in accompanying others in prayer. She is a well-known writer and speaker and is the author of a number of bestselling books in the area of spirituality.

A newsletter came round the other day from our local neighbourhood conservation group. Among other things, it raised the question of light pollution, and suggested, rather alarmingly, that our grandchildren might grow up without ever really being able to see the Milky Way. What an irony, in the age in which human beings have dramatically viewed planet earth from outer space, and the Hubble telescope has given us breathtaking images of the awesome universe in which we live. Yet our children rarely see the night sky in its full glory, because we have strewn our cities with street lights and advertising signs, and even our gardens have been invaded by security beams and floodlights.

Even so, I am still spellbound by the night sky, and I often stand outside on a starry night and simply gaze. Sometimes I feel it's the nearest to God I am ever likely to get. I especially look at the constellation of the Plough, and trace its stars around the frying-pan shape that eventually leads to the position of the Pole Star. Something about standing facing due north speaks to me deeply. I like to imagine a vast invisible axis running through the heart of all creation, and around which all creation, as dreamed into being by God, revolves in perfect balance. I know the universe doesn't quite work like that, but the image is helpful nevertheless.

Then I take it further and imagine that invisible true axis of life running right through our own human hearts too, and I realize how 'tilted' I am— how often out of true with the axis around which I desire my life to be spinning. For me, Jesus of Nazareth is the one who lives in perfect alignment with that true axis of life. That's why I'm a Christian. I want my life to be aligned like that too, and the Christ-story shows a way.

Then I cast my gaze over the other familiar constellations. In the Western world we have learned to identify them by means of classical myths. No doubt most of us have stood under the night sky and tried desperately to recognize some ancient hero or mythical beast in their shapes. Frankly, it has never worked well for me. Maybe I didn't listen in class when classical mythology was on the menu, but there's something about searching for Pegasus or Orion that distracts me from the wonder of it all. It feels like trying to pin down the mystery in our own kind of knowledge.

Imagine my delight, therefore, when I found myself standing under the skies of the southern hemisphere, gazing up

When I consider your heavens, the work of your fingers, the moon and the stars you have set in their courses, What are mortals, that you should be mindful of them? Mere human beings, that you should seek them out? You have made them a little lower than the angels; you adorn them with glory and honour.

FROM PSALM 8

at the Milky Way from a very different point of view. The great river of stars swept unbroken across the heavens, from horizon to horizon, above a desert landscape. The darkness was absolute, the stillness profound. As I was doing my 'western thing' and searching for the shape of the southern cross, which indicates the location of due south, I noticed a distinctive patch of darkness I had never seen before in the sweep of our galaxy. As I watched, it seemed to resemble the shape of a vast bird.

My aboriginal companion came to my aid. 'Aboriginal people,' she explained, 'find meaning in the dark spaces of the skies, rather than in the

... take a few minutes to stand and gaze

patterns of the stars.' We gazed together at the particular dark shape above us, resembling an emu, and resonant with its own meanings through which aboriginal spirituality tells the God-story. It made deep sense to me. It reminded me that I spend huge amounts of energy trying to derive meaning from the teeming events of my life, and thread a story from all the shapes of my experience, but at a deeper level I know that all the while God is growing God's mystery in the empty spaces of my heart.

Just as we drench our world in artificial light, so too we clog up our lives with achievements and attachments that have no permanent value. In doing so, we might be missing the heart of the matter, where God is dreaming the fullness of creation into being. As we strive so hard to map our own meanings on to

life, we may be missing much deeper and eternal meanings, that are only to be intuited in darkness and emptiness.

God comes to birth in a virginal womb—a place of life-giving darkness and receptive emptiness. God comes to birth in an unfurnished shed—in our own inner poverty. The place where we are most needy and most open is the place where we are most likely to recognize God's transforming power and love. But the God who comes to birth in our own receptive emptiness also asks to walk with us, revealing meaning in our lives and the events of every day and weaving our own stories into the creation story and the God-story.

The night skies can help us connect to both these realities—the recognition of God's gestation in the empty spaces of our own hearts, and the challenge to allow God to become incarnate in our lived experience, to tell the God-story in and through our own stories, so that all creation might grow a notch closer to the fullness of the Kingdom.

Our destiny may not be 'written in the stars', but perhaps the stars can give us some clues about where to look for God in the unfolding stories of our lives—if we have the courage to switch off our lesser lights from time to time, and take a few minutes to stand and gaze. ∎

Saint Francis for today

Rosemary Went is a Third Order Franciscan with an MTh in Applied Theology. She enjoys writing poetry. Together with her husband John, the Bishop of Tewkesbury, she leads Quiet Days for BRF.

When we think of creation and delight in the natural world, our minds turn very quickly to St Francis. Into our mind's eye comes the picture of Francis and the birds. We can recall snippets of his words brought to mind through hymns we know. But what can we learn from a life lived at such a different time, in such a different place.

Francis was born in 1182 in Assisi, Italy, and lived there until his death in 1226. Although he only lived to 44, he certainly knew what it was like to live life in the fast lane. He was an exciting person to be around because he generated new ideas and new experiences, which he shared enthusiastically with others. What is even more exciting is that we have been able to assimilate many of his ideas today in all sorts of ways as we reflect on his life and teaching.

Francis' change of lifestyle came as a complete surprise to him. He was brought up in a rich household, wanting to fight and achieve knightly honour. This was the time of the Crusades. After receiving a vision, he felt (in the words of his biographer, Bonaventure), 'the Lord touch his heart filling it with such surpassing sweetness

What is even more exciting is that we have been able to assimilate many of his ideas today

that he could neither speak nor move'.[1] He was found in a trance, worshipping God. He went through a time of withdrawal from society, praying to find out what God wanted him to do. At the church of San Damiano he heard a voice saying 'Francis, go and repair my church.'[2]

Here was a man who challenged the church of his day

His heart, so full of love for God, was drawn to the needs of others

He thought that this meant rebuilding it. At the Portiuncula, one of the churches he rebuilt, he heard Matthew 10:7–10, where God called him never to turn back.

Francis' life was bound up with the death and resurrection of our Lord and he received the stigmata (crucifixion wounds) on his body. This was confirmation for him of his relationship with Christ and was a seal of God's approval for him. Many initiatives flowed from him during his life. He created the Order of Franciscans for his brothers in Christ, the Poor Clares for women, and the Third Order for lay people. Here was a man who challenged the church of his day, the simple style of his 'orders' contrasting wildly with the established church. But you don't have to belong to an order to be a Franciscan. Francis offers us an exploration into our faith in a Franciscan way.

Love in action

Before Francis' life came under the hand of God, he couldn't cope with the poor and the needy. Then, living in Christ, he washed the feet of lepers, kissed their wounds, bandaged their sores and embraced them. During his first pilgrimage to Rome, he gave away a purseful of his father's money to the poor; then he exchanged clothes with a beggar. His heart, so full of love for God, was drawn to the needs of others and led to daily acts of practical care and concern for those in need.

Every step a prayer

Francis loved to pray, anywhere and everywhere. He also believed in praying at any time. He loved praying with people and at other times retreated to be with God on his own. He advocated creating special places for prayer outdoors and indoors. The warm climate in Italy made it easy for him to be outdoors. But we can walk and pray whatever the weather, enjoying the different seasons. Francis loved to pray himself into passages of scripture. One example of this is that he would enter into the Christmas story and kneel in wonder at the crib. He took his whole life to God in prayer; none of it was left out.

Finding balance

For Francis, his 'doing' as well as his 'being' in Christ was very important to him. God called him to 'do'—to care, to love, to spread the good news of Christ to others. He called him to 'be' in Christ through his prayer life. 'Doing' and 'being' are wrapped up together in Francis' desire for God's peace in his life and in the lives of others—so much so that he says to God, 'Make me a channel of your peace'. This wonderful prayer/poem moulds the two ideals of 'doing' and 'being' together and reflects the way in which Francis felt Christ expected him to live.

A spirituality of creation

Francis' joy in God's created world enveloped him. If he knew about what was happening to the ozone layer today, he would be sad and angry too. His canticles capture his sheer delight in creation and his praise for its Creator. Francis is known to have talked or preached to flowers and trees. All living things worked together for Francis in his perception of God's world. He loved watching what went on in nature, praising God for the joy of life in seeing an ant on a leaf or a bee buzzing in the flowers. Sometimes Francis is spoken of as being the first ecologist—the first person to care for the earth in this special way. His deepest joy was in this spirituality of creation. Francis combined a deep reverence for creation with a deep love for the crucified Lord. ■

NOTES

1   Brother Ramon, *Franciscan Spirituality*, SPCK, p. 37.
2   *Franciscan Spirituality*, p. 38

Canticle of the Sun

Most high, most great and good Lord, to you belong praises, glory
and every blessing; to you alone do they belong, most high God.

May you be blessed, my Lord, for the gift of all your creatures
and especially for our brother sun, by whom the day is enlightened.
He is radiant and bright, of great splendour, bearing witness to you,
O my God.

May you be blessed, my Lord, for our sister the moon and the stars;
you have created them in the heavens, fair and clear.

May you be blessed, my Lord, for our brother the wind, for the air,
for cloud and calm, for every kind of weather, for through them
you sustain all creatures.

May you be blessed, my Lord, for our sister water, which is very
useful, humble, pure and precious.

May you be blessed, my Lord, for our brother fire, bright, noble and
beautiful, untamable and strong, by whom you illume the night.

May you be blessed, my Lord, for our mother the earth, who
sustains and nourishes us, who brings forth all kinds of fruit, herbs
and brightly coloured flowers.

FRANCIS OF ASSISI

Creation's
window on suffering

Jean Watson is a writer and speaker. Her love of fiction inspires much of her work, as does her experience of bereavement. Jean lives in Sevenoaks, Kent.

Suffering can open a window in the closed wall of your life and allow you to glimpse the new pasture of creativity on which you are called to walk and wander

JOHN O'DONOHUE

One of the windows that suffering has opened for me has shown me nature at new depths—though not immediately after my bereavement, when the anguish was raw. Then, on the worst days, the beauty and continuity of the natural world seemed heartless, like an affront to my feelings. 'Pack up the moon and dismantle the sun'—this response of the mourner in one of Auden's poems seemed rather extreme, but I could identify with his desire to make time stand still. As the days went by, however, nature played a big part in my journey through grief.

Beauty is God's handwriting—a wayside sacrament

RALPH WALDO EMERSON

Nature's beauty

I tremble with pleasure when I think that on the very day of my leaving prison the laburnum and lilac will be blooming in the gardens.
OSCAR WILDE

Right after my husband's sudden death, the autumn colours were indescribably stunning. At first, on my better days, they brought me only very painful joy but subsequently and increasingly I was able to drink in, like nectar, nature's colours and shapes, sounds, scents and textures, and experience less ambiguous delight.

But there is more to beauty than the joy it brings to our senses, healing and inspiring as that is. 'Beauty,' writes Kathleen Raine, 'is the real aspect of things when seen aright and with the eyes of love.' And Delmore Schwartz suggests: 'If you can look at anything long enough, you will rejoice at the miracle of love.'

So beauty is reality—the way things really are or should be—and a miracle of love. But we need the eyes of love, eyes that look long enough, in order to be able to see this.

How do we develop those eyes and that kind of looking? I suggest it is by allowing our suffering to be experienced fully, reflected on and grown through. This can teach us to look long and deeply, with heart, imagination and spirit. Then we are able to gaze at nature's harmony, order and pattern and glimpse a meaningful universe, a creative intelligence; to bask in its loveliness and feel love and a yearning for its perfect, divine source.

Nature's seasons

There is a… season for every activity under heaven.
ECCLESIASTES 3:1 (NIV)

I see nature's seasons as cycles of growth and change, analogous in many ways to the seasons of life and of the heart. Spring bespeaks the freshness and happiness, the adventurousness and exuberance of youth; summer the more mature satisfactions, choices and enjoyments from busyness, hands-on involvement, achievement; autumn the deeper, subtler joys of fulfilment, reaping, stepping back and slowing down to savour and reflect on life.

And then there's winter—often dark and colourless, when things seem dead and conditions are harsh; but in reality a great deal is going on below the surface, though it will take time for this to show in leaf, fruit and flower. Similarly, in times of pain and difficulty the real work, real changes, can be going on quietly, beyond appearances, deep inside us; and if we see them through, we will one day enjoy the outcome—new life, renewal. Living out a 'season', even a dark one that we would never have chosen, can be the prelude to moving out into new opportunities and challenges.

Nature's peace

Nature's silence, stillness and patience speak to me of the deep and precious, shy and subtle insights which can reward those who know how to wait and listen, how to become sufficiently still and receptive. Socrates wrote that the unreflected life is not worth living—and certainly I have found that learning to meditate and contemplate in the presence of God who is 'in here' as well as 'out there' can be gently life-changing. I am very much a learner, but an eager one, in developing what Henri Nouwen called 'a quiet inner centre' out of which I can 'listen' at new depths to all that is around and within me, and grow in understanding and awareness.

Nature's 'healing'

Patiently the earth's wounds close.
The womb heals of its sons
As bark over a torn branch grows.
KATHLEEN RAINE

An emotional wound can grow a scar, which will gradually fade and perhaps even disappear—assuming the original injury was properly tended and treated; otherwise, of course, the scar will sooner or later burst open to reveal the sore or suppuration beneath.

As the days went by, nature played a big part in my journey through grief

I am increasingly assured that suffering, cruelty and chaos will not have the last word

Grafting—the process by which broken branches can be grafted on to growing ones and be as strong as they were before or even stronger—this, too, has parallels with emotional healing. Lily Pincus, a guru on healthy mourning, suggests how this may happen: 'Only when the lost person has been internalized and becomes part of the bereaved, a part which can be integrated with his own personality and enriches it, is the mourning process complete.' And Jean Vanier, whose life and work with vulnerable people makes him specially qualified to speak about suffering and healing, sees God as very much involved in the process:

Our brokenness is the wound
Through which the full power of God
Can penetrate our being
And transfigure us in him.

Nature's patterns of life and growth

Seeds are sown in the dark earth and, for a while, nothing appears to be happening, but underneath the surface, plenty is going on and in the end the thrust towards the light and the sun succeeds and a thing of beauty is born. All things being equal, it grows, thrives and gives of itself, until it is time to return to the soil and the dark and start the whole process over again. I'm sure others will see different parallels here, but for me these patterns speak of the way God works in nature and in our lives; and of our ultimate hope, based on Christ's death and resurrection, that we too will pass from death to a new and different life.

Nature's cruelty

Meanwhile, what are we to make of nature 'red in tooth and claw'—its wildness, savagery and apparent cruelty? Of evil and suffering in human life? Specifically in my human life? Of course we are all flawed but perhaps, like Job, we feel with justice that we don't deserve the barrage of suffering that we are having to endure, while other 'sinners' appear to be getting off lightly.

A choice faces us. We can decide that there's no justice, and that meaninglessness and randomness rule;

or we can engage in deeper looking and listening, trying to see a bit more of the picture and work out what this tells us. The testimony of many is that when we press on in our honest dialogue with God, ourselves, others, life and the world about us, these

We are made whole at the broken places

ERNEST HEMINGWAY

> God has written messages of hope even into our flawed and suffering world

encounters and relationships reassure us in all kinds of small and subtle ways. The big mysteries remain and complete explanations elude us. At least, that is my experience so far. But I am increasingly assured that suffering, cruelty and chaos will not have the last word, for God has written messages of hope even into our flawed and suffering world, at all kind of levels—creational, physiological, psychological, you name it… We can continue to discover these messages and to trust that answers to life's mysteries and difficult questions do exist and that these will one day be seen to be good, loving and beautiful.

Nature's designer

Nature is the living, visible garment of God.
GOETHE

Celtic Christianity reminds us of the importance of humans reconnecting with nature. Some of their writers tell us poetically and memorably about creation's intricacy and interconnectedness, its regularity and radiance. These attributes can delight our senses and increase our physical health and well-being; stimulate our minds and inspire our imaginations and creativity; give us new insights into ourselves and the world. They can raise our spirits in both senses of that phrase—bringing us joy and hope in the midst of sadness, tacitly pointing us to God and encouraging us to practise the presence of God in the whole of our lives now, as a prelude to full and perfect union with him and all who love him in the new, perfect and (unimaginably!) painless new heaven and earth. ■

'Let the earth bring forth living creatures of every kind'

Camille Saint-Saëns: The Carnival of the Animals

Gordon Giles is a vicar in north-west London, previously based at St Paul's Cathedral, where his work involved musical and liturgical responsibilities. He is trained in music, philosophy and theology. This article is an abridged extract from his much-praised book, 'The Harmony of Heaven'.

And God said, 'Let the earth bring forth living creatures
of every kind: cattle and creeping things and wild
animals of the earth of every kind.' And it was so. God
made the wild animals of the earth of every kind, and
the cattle of every kind, and everything that creeps
upon the ground of every kind. And God saw that it
was good. Then God said, 'Let us make humankind in
our image, according to our likeness; and let them
have dominion over the fish of the sea, and over the
birds of the air, and over the cattle, and over all the
wild animals of the earth, and over every creeping
thing that creeps upon the earth.' So God created
humankind in his image, in the image of God he
created them; male and female he created them. God
blessed them, and God said to them, 'Be fruitful and
multiply, and fill the earth and subdue it; and have
dominion over the fish of the sea and over the birds
of the air and over every living thing that moves
upon the earth.'
GENESIS 1:24–28 (NRSV)

Let the earth bring forth living creatures of every kind

When we think of creation, we are often drawn to the wide diversity and range of God's creatures, living and extinct. The unique wealth and beauty of the many kinds of creature on this earth delight us, and encourage us in the belief that our rotating planet is in some way special and marked out by God as the object of his creative love. God's creation is not just a range of creatures, though; it is also what those creatures do and how they live.

The skills that we have are all part of God's creative gift, and so it is only right that we should see language, art, friendship and love as part of God's created order. Thus, when we encounter works of art reflecting on the beauties of creation, we are doubly inspired. When human creativity can reflect on creation, and can do so with humour and delight, we are triply blessed, and, as in the case of Camille Saint-Saëns' *Grande Fantasie Zoologique* 'Le Carnival des Animaux', we can rejoice even more at the way in which the composer manages to place humanity and human creativity within the context of divine creation.

Saint-Saëns (1835–1921) was organist at the Madeleine Church in Paris, and is known for his Third 'Organ' Symphony, piano and violin concertos, and for this delightful and immensely popular suite for piano duet and orchestra, written in 1886. He would have been rather embarrassed at the success that his zoological fantasy has had. For while on one level it is a delightful portrayal of God's creation—a happy procession of creatures lovingly illustrated—it is also a satirical work, mercilessly parodying his contemporaries in a more than light-hearted way. The French composers Offenbach (who wrote the famous 'can-can') and Berlioz have their music parodied as the tortoises 'dance' the former (very slowly!) and the elephants stomp all over the latter's 'Sylphs' Dance'! Mendelssohn and Rossini get similar treatment, alongside popular songs of the day. With a certain humility of humour Saint-Saëns also abuses one of his own works, the *Danse Macabre*; this, in its portrayal of rattling bones springing to life (a resonance of Ezekiel's Valley of Dry Bones, perhaps), is well suited to a xylophonic joke.

The greatest humour, and the greatest significance, is to be found in the portrayal of pianists. Saint-Saëns sees them as a species of animal, up to their tricks, parading their virtuosity and doing their exercises. Many pianists, whether successful or not, will remember the bane of early music lessons—of playing scales and learning fingerings—and may well have felt like some kind of performing monkey in doing so. Saint-Saëns captures this spirit of piano practice delightfully, and while his tongue is firmly in his cheek, this portrayal of the human animal making music is also indicative of a profound truth.

There is a story about the great pianist Artur Rubenstein, who was acting as adjudicator in a piano competition. A young hopeful, performing at a high

O God of love, through whom all things living are made, we give you thanks for the beauties of your creation, and especially for the skills and gifts you bestow on musicians and performers. By your Holy Spirit, help us to live your gospel and practise our faith, that we may reflect your perfect love revealed in the death and resurrection of your Son, our Saviour Jesus Christ. Amen.

PRAYER

... in Christ all creation shall be redeemed

ROMANS 8:18–23

level, played his recital pieces, and afterwards, with a mixture of pride and apprehension, said to the great man: 'Maestro, how did I do? Did you like my playing?' Rubenstein looked at the nervous pianist, and with a wry smile said: 'There were too many right notes!'

How easy it is to let technical brilliance get in the way of human expression and interpretation of the music. Technique is a means to music, not an end in itself. Saint-Saëns is saying the same kind of thing when he parodies the technical exercises which pupils were expected to learn. Such an approach to music is like the kind of legalistic approach to the law that we find Jesus criticizing in the Pharisees (Luke 11:37–52). Strict adherence to the Law of God but without emotion, without love, is not what the Christian faith is about. Yet we are not called to abandon the Law, any more than a musician is told to stop practising scales and arpeggios. We never 'graduate' from God's Law, even if we find, as time goes by, that it becomes part of the fabric of our music and our life, and we instinctively follow it. But even then, because we are only human, we can slip up, and either play a wrong note here and there, or else play so many right notes that we lose the plot of love.

As we approach God, seeking to be made perfect, through Christ we remember that we are sinners but we are also aware that in Christ all creation shall be redeemed (Romans 8:18–23) in one final, technically brilliant, and creatively beautiful revelation of God's glory. ■

> Strict adherence to the Law of God but without emotion, without love, is not what the Christian faith is about

For further reading: Genesis 6:18–20, Luke 11:37–52
For listening: All or part of Saint-Saëns' *The Carnival of the Animals*

Gardens and gardening

This meditation is taken from Transforming the Ordinary *by John Henstridge (BRF, 2004). John is involved with the Guildford Diocese Parish Development team, and is a Vocations Advisor. He is currently doing an MA in Christian Spirituality at Sarum College.*

FROM THE BIBLE

GENESIS 2:5—3:24; MATTHEW 26:36—46; JOHN 20:1–18

There are two different stories of God's creation in Genesis (1:1—2:4 and 2:5—3:24). The second one places the humans in a garden. These accounts embody marvellous truths: God's world is good, wonderfully good; he has made all things well, with abundant beauty and abundant resources. Humankind is made in God's image, a kind of representative of God to care for his world.

Sadly, humankind lets God down all too often. We have marred the image of God in us; we have not always cared for his world as we should. There is beauty in the truths of these two stories but also sadness.

There is another garden just outside Jerusalem—the garden of Gethsemane. Here Jesus came with his disciples after the Passover supper they had shared. Here he moved away from his disciples and, in human agony, he prayed, 'Abba, Father, for you all things are possible; remove this cup from me; yet not what I will but what you will.'

He gave his will to his heavenly Father in obedience for the salvation of all humankind.

On the Sunday after he was crucified, a third garden witnessed the most marvellous events, for on Mary Magdalene's early morning visit to the tomb, she made the amazing discovery that the great stone sealing the entrance to the tomb had been rolled away. She ran immediately to tell the disciples.

Later, after Peter and John had been and gone, Mary met the Lord, but at first failed to recognize him. Jesus only spoke her name: 'Mary!' And Mary, overjoyed, fell at his feet. The day of desolation had become the most wonderful day ever, the day of resurrection!

MEDITATION

Imagine you are going out into your garden or a garden of your imagination on, say, a May morning. Picture yourself there, as you stand and look, or wander around. You see how plants are growing, what needs doing next; you enjoy the beauty of the fresh flowers. The garden is vibrant with life. Even weeds are growing at an amazing rate.

Now bring to mind the garden of creation. God, in his abundant love, has made all things well. There is marvellous beauty, and there is joy and peace.

The first garden is the most glorious place, outshining all other gardens. We rest for a moment, breathing in its loveliness and tranquillity.

> **He gave his will to his heavenly Father in obedience for the salvation of all humankind.**

But the beauty is marred by a sadness—the disobedience of humankind. Alas that we despoil God's marvellous creation—both his world and also our own nature.

Alone we can do nothing to right the wrongs we have done. We can only turn to God and seek his forgiveness and his grace.

Back in our own garden, we take out our spade and fork, and start to dig out weeds, and turn the soil over ready to plant. It is heavy work. We pause often to rest and stretch.

The weeds are deep-rooted; they have got a hold—a bit like the sinfulness of humankind. But God loves us; he hears our pleas for forgiveness and grace. And he has come to our world in the person of Jesus Christ.

Now we picture Jesus in the garden of Gethsemane. We see his agony as he faces the prospect of terrible suffering and death. We try to pray with him, to stay alert, awake.

Lord, if only we could do something. We would share your agony, but we are helpless. We cannot repair the wrongs done by human-kind; we are unable to restore ourselves to the Father. Only your sacrifice can do that.

We adore you for your generous love; we worship you in your total self-giving. May your love cleanse all that is evil in us and in your world.

Back in our garden, we look with satisfaction at the digging we have done. Now the ground is clean and clear of weeds, ready for fresh planting. We stand back with contentment.

There's another garden fresh with the early morning. People come and go to visit the tomb in that garden. First we see Mary and observe her surprise and alarm to see that the tomb is open—the stone covering it rolled away.

We see Peter and John come running; we watch them looking into the tomb, and see their wonder that it is empty. Then they too leave.

We see Mary return, crying because she believes someone has stolen the body of her Lord.

Then the biggest surprise of all. Jesus the risen Lord is standing there. What joy!

Mary responds to him, thinking he's the gardener; and he says—as only he can say—her name: 'Mary!'

We share her bliss as she falls at his feet. We share the joy of new creation. Jesus has restored the glory of God's image in humankind. He has overcome sin and evil.

The treasure of God's creation, marred in that first garden, has been recreated and revealed in this garden.

Glory and praise be to the risen Lord. Alleluia. ∎

Lord, we thank you for the beauty of your world, and especially for gardens. We pray that we may find the love and peace of Jesus in gardens, and remember the joy of his resurrection.

PRAYER

A holy space:

Intermission at St Saviour's

The Revd Rob Gillion is Vicar of two parishes in Chelsea—St Simon Zelotes, a Prayer Book Society church, and St Saviour's and Intermission, which has a contemporary feel, focusing on the arts. He is Adviser in Evangelism for the Bishop of Kensington, and a member of the Archbishop's College of Evangelists. Rob used to be a professional actor: he now enjoys working with various teams presenting the gospel of Christ through theatre and the arts.

In his stimulating book *The Empty Space*, theatre director Peter Brook calls the stage 'Holy Theatre'. As an actor and priest, this description resonates with me, for I want the church to offer a holy space. It is because of that strong desire that we opened a once-redundant church in Walton Place, London, that had been 'dark' for seven years.

I love the comment made by the Chief Rabbi, Jonathan Sachs, recently. He offered a perfect answer to consumerism—the Sabbath. He described the consumerist society as 'a place where we are conscious of what we do not have; whereas the Sabbath space makes us conscious of what we do have'.

In these desperate times of terror and rumours of war, there is such a desire for peace, and we have found people longing for a space—a space to find solace and care, and a time just to be. That is why we called the new project 'Intermission at St Saviour's'. It is to be a place to pause in this troubled life. In theatre terms, an

An imaginative attempt to engage in community and faith-sharing through prayer, worship and the arts

Artwork © Billy
www.elizabethalan.com

intermission is a chance to stretch your legs and be refreshed with a drink or an ice-cream, and to discuss the play and reflect with others before continuing the story and the journey.

That's not a bad description of a church. Times of intermission are important—in fact, vital to everyone's life. We should have many intermissions, not just one.

So this was much, much more than a project just to save a church building. It is an imaginative attempt to engage in community and faith-sharing through prayer, worship and the arts—'a fresh expression of church', perhaps. In the process there has been a merging of the traditional with the contemporary, and a growing expectation that being church might be radically different. Within this holy space, artists are encouraged to express their faith in Christ through their gifts.

Story-rich church

St Saviour's has already become a story-rich church. In its first few years we have entertained a wonderful diversity of actors, artists, dancers and musicians, who have breathed new life into it. I'm not sure whether anyone expected what has developed, but when the Holy Spirit flew down from the rafters and danced above our heads (literally), we knew that we would see some risk-taking!

During the week of the London Fashion Show, a couple of designers turned up to worship with us and asked if they could stage a fashion show. We said 'Yes'. So began a real adventure. The show was entitled 'Faith and Fashion'. We built a catwalk, and twelve models showed off the fashions. I then preached about the clothes that Christ encourages us to wear—'Clothes of compassion, kindness, humility, gentleness and patience... and over all these virtues put on love which binds them together in perfect unity'. It was so exciting.

Every Thursday lunchtime, around 20 people gather for a time of meditation and reflection. Those who come are from our own worshipping community, artists who are with us at the time and the local working community, especially including some staff from Harrods (our church is just at the back of this store). Together we explore the creativity of God through prayer and reflection, often focusing on a recent art exhibition or performance, recognizing the presence of Christ.

Out of my relationship with the staff of Harrods I have been invited to be, as my Bishop commented, 'Vicar' of Harrods. I am there to help in pastoral care for all the staff and to support the Christians in the store. Together we have recently staged an Alpha course for them at St Saviour's.

As well as meditation and prayer there are other opportunities for exciting vitality and exuberance through theatrical presentations. God is mischievous and has a wonderful sense of humour, and that is also cause for celebration.

Together we explore the creativity of God through prayer and reflection

Sunday is our time as a 'regular' parish church for quiet meditative worship where we break bread as a family. Being asked what churchmanship we represent poses a bit of a challenge, but we have agreed on quietly contemporary with traditional undertones! We often meet in a circle, knowing that all of us are of equal importance to our community and to God, and the children of the church are placed firmly in the middle of our circle.

The real joy of a holy space is that the activity within it refreshes the Spirit

We have engaged a resident artist each year, who is invited to reflect something of the ministry and mission of the Church, as well as offering them an opportunity to exhibit their work. Our first artist in residence was Carla Moss. Her exhibition at the end of her year was entitled 'Inside Out'. It was presented during the Chelsea Flower Show, and involved covering the church floor in wood bark. It was really 'alive' and it took some time to transform it into the sweet smell of a forest. Over the weeks, it became a playground for children as well as a challenge to those who walked through it to worship. For us it was bringing the world into the church and transforming it. Carla reflected that the church is somewhere where we can bring all our personal rubbish, leave what needs to be left, change what needs to be changed into something beautiful, and then be sent back out into the world stronger for it. The key word is transformation.

The first two years have been full of activities. Within the last six months we have hosted seven art exhibitions, a production of Shakespeare's *Measure for Measure*, two Oscar Wilde short stories performed by The Grace Project, an exploration of faith through dance and multi-media with Japanese postgraduates, a book launch, visits from BRF, the Quiet Garden Trust and the Jane Austen Society, the Bishop's Vision Day, and Hill House School evensongs. We also hold monthly meetings with Christians in Journalism, monthly prayer mornings with the 'Art's Warriors', Arts Centre Group gatherings and meetings, resourcing and training days, 'Focus on Faith' evenings, plus our own Bible study and church celebrations, 'Alpha' and 'Essence' courses.

If you find the thought of all this activity exhausting, be assured that the real joy of a holy space is that the activity within it refreshes the Spirit. I am a great believer in creative partnerships and I believe that our love of the arts and our response to the artist bring about a synergy that resonates with the mission at the heart of the Church. ∎

May I encourage you, if you come to London, to pop in and see us and enjoy the peace of our holy space. You will be very welcome.
Find out more at www.intermission.org.uk.

Why go on retreat?

*Fleur Dorrell is head of spirituality and prayer for the Mothers'
Union and is an experienced retreat attender and leader.*

Jesus needed to be alone from time to time. We see
from the Gospels that he withdrew on several
occasions to pray alone and to talk to his Father.

The idea of retreating and withdrawing is not new.
Elijah and the Old Testament prophets frequently
spent time alone, praying, fasting and listening to the
word of God. John the Baptist regularly went into the
desert to pray.

Retreats rekindle
our awareness of
God's presence
in our everyday
lives

What is a retreat today?

A retreat is a period of quiet reflection that provides us with space, silence and time to deepen our relationship with God. It can be anything from an afternoon to a number of months and can be made in partial or total silence.

Each of us needs to find a balance between *doing* and *being*. Retreats revive this balance within us as they rekindle our awareness of God's presence in our everyday lives. By removing ourselves from our usual commitments and daily life, we become free to be inwardly still, and to think, feel and pray.

Through making a retreat, we may feel challenged to make changes in our lives. Retreats can help us to face our fears and provide us with new ways forward. Alternatively they can affirm us in what we are doing and thinking. Our life's goal is to get to know who we are and who God is to us, so retreats can be viewed as small steps along this journey. Spending time in God's presence will always transform us.

Retreats are extremely popular right now, as the world has become so busy. People are crying out for space and time purely to be. The good news is that there are so many different types of retreats that one can be found to suit most personalities or needs.

Our souls are nourished in extraordinary ways through retreats. What often seems absolutely terrifying in our life can be given a new perspective and a more manageable framework when we place all our burdens in God's hands. Retreats help us to be ready to listen to him in focused ways.

The most effective listening to God is achieved when our silence allows us to be more receptive to him. To do this we need few distractions. Reflecting, meditating, mulling, thinking, feeling, searching,

In my retreats I try to explore new ways of thinking and seeing God and our spirituality

To do this I have used scripture, poetry, art, pottery, silence, writing, music, drama, walking, writing and meditations

praying, seeking, listening and travelling are attempts of the soul to perceive the divine. The essence of a retreat is to grasp at the divine and to love it from within, to embrace the divine with all our pain and grief and to offer them to God's greater love.

Spiritual direction

There are times in your life when you need specific guidance. Spiritual direction or guidance in prayer can help you with this. It is the befriending of a person's soul. It is travelling together but with one of the travellers gently leading the other towards God. Spiritual direction is the pure act of love and service to another individual; its most important components are trust, prayer, listening and desiring God's love for that person. It is like a butterfly—easily crushed if mishandled but able to fly away if not held down.

A director's task is to listen and, by God's grace, to hear what the love of God is wanting in this person for their fulfilment. A skilled director will be able to listen intently and know the right questions to ask, the right responses or images to use, to help the person to go one step further, to dare to trust and to want to understand better. A good director will not pin down the wings of the person's soul but will allow it to fly freely in the air that is God's love.

If you have never been on a retreat, then try it. It may be one of the most important decisions you will ever make. ■

> There are endless possibilities to re-centre our hearts on God and reveal new depths to our souls

For further information about retreats, contact The Retreat Association, The Central Hall, 256 Bermondsey Street, London SE1 3UJ. Tel: 0207 357 7736. E-mail:info@retreats.org.uk. Website: www.retreats.org.uk

Thanks for this day

This meditation is taken from 'Quiet Spaces' by Patricia Wilson (BRF, 2003). Patricia is an author and speaker who conducts business seminars across Canada and the USA, specializing in communication topics. She lives on an island off the coast of Nova Scotia, Canada.

Thank you for this day and for its endless possibilities

CALMING

I will praise you, O Lord, with all my heart;
I will tell of all your wonders.
I will be glad and rejoice in you;
I will sing praise to your name,
O Most High.

PSALM 9:1–2

CENTRING

Cup your hands and imagine that you are holding a small seed in them. When you look at the seed, you have no idea what will come from it: whether it will be a beautiful blossom; a small, insignificant weed; or a giant tree. This seed symbolizes the possibilities that lie in this day.

PRAYING

Here is today, O God.

I don't know what this day will bring, although I like to think that I do. I have my schedule, my to-do list filled in, my agenda duly noted. I like to think that I have this day under my control.

But I know that's not how most days go.

I know that today I will be surprised by sorrows, joys, and challenges.

I know that today I will face both problems and adventures.

I know that today may be just an ordinary day, or it might be the most extraordinary day of my life.

And I know that you are the only one who knows what lies ahead. So I offer you this day.

(Raise your cupped hands and imagine giving the small seed to God.)

Here is today, O God. I give it to you, trusting that you will take whatever happens in this day and use it for your glory. I trust that whatever happens today, you will be with me.

Thank you for this day and for its endless possibilities. Thank you that I can face this day with you.

Here is today, O God:
a part of all the days we have spent together,
   a part of all the days to come,
     a part of who I am and where I am on
      my journey,
       a part of the plan that you have
        for me.

Take this day. Use it to your glory. Thank you, God.

LISTENING

Though it is the smallest of all your seeds, yet when it grows, it is the largest of garden plants and becomes a tree, so that the birds of the air come and perch in its branches.

MATTHEW 13:32

RETURNING

Remind yourself that you have offered today to God. Remember lifting that small seed that represents today and giving it to God to be used as God sees fit.

Creation and creativity

These prayers are written by Jenny Biggar, who is a BRF trustee. She works as a secretary and is a trained counsellor. Music making, cooking and writing are among her main enjoyments.

There are various different ways in which you can use these pages. The prayers are designed so that they can be used in addition to your usual pattern, as a way of weaving this issue's theme into all the other things we offer to God. You may decide to use these prayers for one week, or you may like to repeat them week after week.

Praying with all our senses can be especially helpful as we reflect on God's creation. Here are suggestions for different items to stimulate prayer.

- Lavender, rosemary or any herb with a smell you like.
- Fresh, cool water—pour it, feel it, listen to it, drink it.
- A photograph of a place or person of special significance.

- Some awe-inspiring music—
  Haydn's *The Creation*, for example.
- A smooth pebble, or textured shells,
  a pine cone—anything that feels
  interesting.
- A food or drink you really love.
  Savour each sip or taste.

⁜

Sunday

God said, 'Let there be light',
and there was light.

*Heavenly Father, you made light—in
your creation, and in our hearts and
minds as they respond to you.*

*I am sorry for the times I have
turned away from your light. Please
forgive me.*

*Thank you for always being here
with me, no matter what. Please help
me to be more aware of you and allow
your light to shine in and through me.*

*Heavenly Father, I pray for those who
work to enlighten others. Encourage
those who tell of your good news,
inspire those who teach, guide and bless
those who care for the blind and those
facing any kind of darkness.*

*Heavenly Father, may I walk in your
light and more closely with you this day
and every day. Amen.*

⁜

Monday

God called the expanse 'sky'.

*Heavenly Father, your sky is
overarching, immense, inescapable, like
your love, and it is part of the order you
have made so carefully.*

*I am sorry for the times I have
ignored your care and damaged your
created order. Please forgive me.*

*Thank you for always being here with
me, no matter what. Please help me to
be more aware of you and the great
variety of beauty you have created.*

*Heavenly Father, I pray for those who
try to express such beauty—painters,
poets, composers. Give them a renewed
vision of your greatness and enable
them to convey this to others.*

*Heavenly Father, may I be more and
more aware of your overarching love
this day and every day. Amen.*

⁜

Tuesday

God called the dry ground 'land'.

*Heavenly Father, you have made the
way firm under my feet. All manner of
things green and growing surround me,
a feast for my eyes as well as food for
my body.*

I am sorry for the times I have taken your provision for granted. Please forgive me.

Thank you for always being here with me, no matter what. Please help me to be more aware of you and trust and depend on you more.

Heavenly Father, I pray for those who work the land to provide people with food. Give farmers and gardeners patience, endurance and wisdom, and a fair price for their produce.

Heavenly Father, may I walk faithfully along your way this day and every day. Amen.

⁘

Wednesday

God made the sun, the moon
and the stars.

Heavenly Father, you made the sun and the moon to separate day and night. All that you do has a loving purpose.

I am sorry for the times when I have doubted you. Please forgive me.

Thank you for always being here with me, no matter what. Please help me to be more aware of you and the way you are working out your purposes.

Heavenly Father, I pray for those who explore and discover new things, and who try to understand. Give them courage and humility, and the ability to

see how each small part fits into the whole.

Heavenly Father, may I recognize the unfolding of your purposes for me this day and every day. Amen.

⁘

Thursday

God made the creatures of the sea
and of the sky.

Heavenly Father, you filled the sea with living creatures and made birds and insects fly. I marvel at how they evolved and developed.

I am sorry for the times when I have not grown to be more like you. Please forgive me.

Thank you for always being here with me, no matter what. Please help me to be more aware of you and willing to adapt to changing circumstances, and to grow through them.

Heavenly Father, I pray for those who help others adapt to difficulties. Give them resourcefulness and imagination and the ability to see each opportunity.

Heavenly Father, may I adapt to the changes you bring, rather than stubbornly resist them, this day and every day. Amen.

❖

Friday

God made animals and humankind.

Heavenly Father, you have made me in your own image, yet I am unique in your creation.

I am sorry for the times when I have not seen your image in others. Please forgive me.

Thank you for always being here with me, no matter what. Please help me to be more aware of you and the reality of you in me.

Heavenly Father, I pray for those who work to bring respect for others. Give courage to those speaking out against injustice and cruelty. Strengthen those who feel unfairly treated or ignored.

Heavenly Father, may I remember that you love each one of us individually, and may I do the same, this day and every day. Amen.

❖

Saturday

God rested from all his work.

Heavenly Father, you saw all you had made and it was very good. It was complete.

I am sorry for the times when I have not done things well or not finished

them. Please forgive me.

Thank you for always being here with me, no matter what. Please help me to be more aware of you and all that you have done so well.

Heavenly Father, I pray for those who cannot rest—parents with sick children, children forced to work too young and too long, those too fearful to stop being busy. Give them your peace.

Heavenly Father, you completed this great work of creation, and your Son cried, 'It is finished!' when his work was done. May I make the time to be with you, and appreciate all you have done for me, this day and every day. Amen. ■

There is only one point at which we can possibly touch the nerve of God's creative action, or experience creation taking place: and that is in our own life. The believer draws his active Christian existence out of the wellspring of divine creation, he prays prayers which become the very act of God's will and his will. Because we have God under the root of our being we cannot help but acknowledge him at the root of the world's being.

AUSTIN FARRAR

The Creator is author of all arts that are truly arts.

JOHN DUNS SCOTUS (1266–1308)

The world is not like a picture painted by an artist centuries ago which now hangs untouchable in a museum. It is more like a work of art in constant process of creation, still in the studio.

ERNESTO CARDENAL

In the midst of our manifold requests, our complaints and our pleas, Christ comes, raises his hands and says to our hearts, 'Peace, be still.'

**'Yahweh, my heart has no lofty ambitions,
my eyes do not look too high.**

**I am not concerned with great affairs or marvels
beyond my scope.
Enough for me to keep my soul tranquil and quiet
Like a child in his mother's arms,
As content as a child that has been weaned.
Israel, rely on Yahweh, now and for always.'**

PSALM 131

Veronica Zundel is a journalist, author and contributor to BRF's 'New Daylight' Bible reading notes. She lives in north London.

Musings of a middle-aged mystic

'I hope this beautiful scene behind me won't be a distraction from our worship,' announced the leader. My mind did one of those boggling things: what on earth did she mean? Behind her, framed by a huge picture window, was a sparkling Finnish lake, surrounded by sun-drenched trees, under a perfect blue summer sky. Just exactly how was this glorious creation supposed to distract us from worshipping its creator?

But she is not alone in her thinking. Right from the day my infant school headmistress intoned, 'Hands together, eyes closed', I have encountered the idea that to meet God it is best to close one's eyes and shut out the world—that 'the things of earth will grow strangely dim' if only we turn our eyes upon Jesus.

Reader, this is not Christianity. It might be Buddhism, or even Hinduism—faiths which teach that the material world is illusion and that the aim of the spiritual path is to escape from this world of temptation and suffering. It might even be a third-century heresy called Manicheanism, which taught that the material world was created by the power of evil and that salvation meant escaping it.

Whatever it is, it is not the religion of the Jesus in whom God took flesh. The 'things of earth' were not at all

Go, eat your bread with enjoyment, and drink your wine with a merry heart

dim for him: he noticed wild flowers, birds, a farmer sowing seed, a woman baking bread—and, like his Father before him, declared them good. Even after his resurrection, he ate bread and fish on the beach with relish (would that be barbecue relish?) to show that he wasn't a wispy ghost.

Christianity is, like Judaism, an earth-centred faith. In fact, it was when it began to stray from its Jewish roots that it acquired all this other-worldly Greek stuff. Fortunately we have not removed from the Bible (as far as I know) the Ecclesiastes who said, 'Go, eat your bread with enjoyment, and drink your wine with a merry heart…' I'll second that.

All right, I admit there is a valid tradition of turning one's back on worldly pleasures to seek God alone. I studied the medieval mystics at university, and was impressed by their message that one had to ignore all created things to know God. But these books were written by monks and nuns, who never had to change a nappy or do the school run. Their spirituality was fine when I was single and childless, but it just doesn't fit any more.

No, I can't be doing with this 'God is in the spiritual realm and we are in the material one' stuff. If God isn't here as I match up socks or deal with tantrums, then God isn't anywhere for me. So I will keep my eyes open as I pray, whether they're open to the glory of a Finnish lake or my sleeping child; and that will be my spiritual worship. ■

We want to hear from you...

Do you write meditation, prayers or poetry? Do you do calligraphy, cartoons or line drawings? Do you take photographs? Quiet Spaces will be all the richer for your input. Maybe our 'Creation and creativity' theme has inspired you to action. Write to us or send an e-mail with your thoughts.

We would also love your feedback to help us to shape future editions, so do let us know what you liked most about this issue and what you would like more of. And, of course, tell us what you would like less of!

In the next issue, our theme will be the journey—the great journeys of the Bible and the significance and power of the journey metaphor in Christian spirituality. We will explore different facets of journeying: setting out, travelling companions, getting lost/finding the way, nourishment on the journey, imagining the destination, arrival... Do send us your thoughts. ■

Contact us at:

Quiet Spaces,
BRF, First Floor,
Elsfield Hall,
15–17 Elsfield Way,
Oxford OX2 8FG

enquiries@brf.org.uk
www.brf.org.uk

Please do not send originals as we will not be able to return them.

QUIET SPACES SUBSCRIPTIONS

Quiet Spaces Vol 1: Creation and Creativity (*available March 2005*)
Quiet Spaces Vol 2: The Journey (*available July 2005*)
Quiet Spaces Vol 3: The Pilgrimage (*available November 2005*)

☐ I would like to give a gift subscription (please complete both name and address sections below)

☐ I would like to take out a subscription myself (complete name and address details only once)

This completed coupon should be sent with appropriate payment to BRF. Alternatively, please write to us quoting your name, address, the subscription you would like for either yourself or a friend (with their name and address), the start date and credit card number, expiry date and signature if paying by credit card.

Gift subscription name _____

Gift subscription address _____

_____

_____ Postcode _____

Please send beginning with the July / November 2005 / March 2006 issue: *(delete as applicable)*

(please tick box)	UK	SURFACE	AIR MAIL
Quiet Spaces	☐ £16.95	☐ £18.45	☐ £20.85

Please complete the payment details below and send your coupon, with appropriate payment to: BRF, First Floor, Elsfield Hall, 15–17 Elsfield Way, Oxford OX2 8FG.

Name _____

Address _____

_____

Postcode _____ Telephone Number _____

Email _____

☐ Please do not email me any information about BRF publications

Method of payment: ☐ Cheque ☐ Mastercard ☐ Visa ☐ Postal Order ☐ Switch

Card no. ☐☐☐☐ ☐☐☐☐ ☐☐☐☐ ☐☐☐☐

Expires ☐☐ ☐☐ Issue no. of Switch card ☐☐☐

Signature _____ Date ___ / ___ / ___

All orders must be accompanied by the appropriate payment.
Please make cheques payable to BRF

PROMO REF: QS1

☐ Please do not send me further information about BRF publications

BRF is a Registered Charity

64